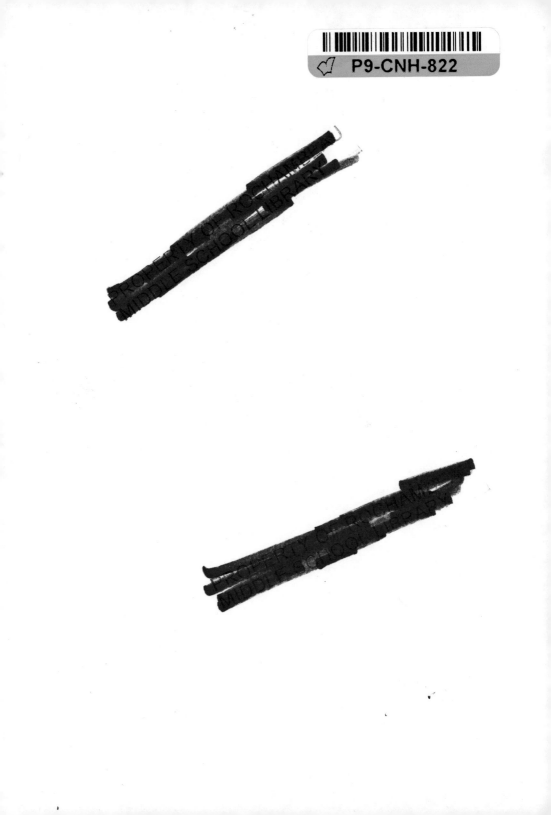

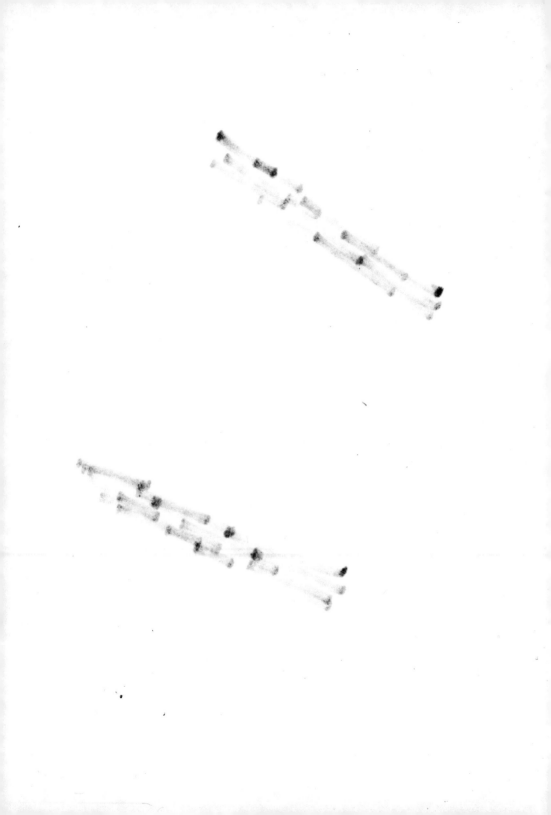

Michael Benson

Lerner Publications Company
Minneapolis

To Lisa, Tekla, and Matthew

Special thanks to Jake Elwell, Norman Jacobs, Sony Music Entertainment, Bert Randolph Sugar, and Tom Warnick.

A&E and **BIOGRAPHY** are trademarks of the A&E Television Networks, registered in the United States and other countries.

Some of the people profiled in this series have also been featured in A&E's acclaimed BIOGRAPHY series, which is available on videocassette from A&E Home Video. Call 1-800-423-1212 to order.

This book is available in two bindings:
Library binding by Lerner Publications Company
Softcover by First Avenue Editions
Divisions of Lerner Publishing Group
241 First Avenue North
Minneapolis, MN 55401 U.S.A.

Website address: www.lernerbooks.com

Library of Congress Cataloging-in-Publication Data

Benson, Michael.
    Gloria Estefan / by Michael Benson.
        p. cm. — (A&E biography)
    Includes discography, bibliographical references, and index.
    Summary: Presents a biography of the Cuban-born singer, composer and entertainer who has recorded such hits as "Into the Light," "Conga," "Turn the Beat Around," and "Reach."
    ISBN 0-8225-4982-4 (alk. paper).
    ISBN 0-8225-9692-X (pbk. : alk. paper)
    1. Estefan, Gloria—Juvenile literature. 2. Singers—United States Biography—Juvenile literature. [1. Estefan, Gloria. 2. Singers.
3. Cuban Americans—Biography. 4. Women—Biography.] I. Title.
II. Series.
MS3930.E85B46 2000
782.42164'092—dc21
[B]   99–36262

Manufactured in the United States of America
1 2 3 4 5 6 - JR – 05 04 03 02 01 00

CONTENTS

Gloria, right, *rides a ferry with actor Edward James Olmos*, left, *on her way to receive a Congressional Medal of Honor in 1993.* •

Chapter **ONE**

BEHIND THE ORANGE BOWL

ON A GRAY OVERCAST DAY IN MAY 1993, Gloria Estefan boarded a ferry destined for Ellis Island in New York. Years earlier, from 1892 to 1924, Ellis Island was the main place where immigrants to the United States were checked and processed before being allowed to pass through to the mainland.

Dressed in a businesslike white suit with a string of pearls, thirty-eight-year-old Gloria Estefan was unlike those earlier immigrants. While most of the people who passed through Ellis Island were poor and unknown, Gloria was famous and wealthy. She had made a fortune with her voice, her songwriting skills, and her concert performances long before she ever set foot on Ellis Island. She had fans all over the world. Moreover, she had shown herself to be a compassionate superstar who contributed to worthy causes. Within the previous year, in addition to releasing a new, groundbreaking compact disc, Gloria had raised money for victims of a devastating hurricane and had served on a committee of the United Nations.

Gloria was one of 150 people summoned to Ellis Island to receive awards on that overcast day in May 1993. All were being recognized for their contributions to the United States. Gloria was given the Ellis Island Congressional Medal of Honor—the highest award the United States gives to a citizen born outside the country. Clearly, she had attained a satisfying life. She was successful, well educated, highly respected, happily married, beautiful, and wealthy.

But life was not always posh for Gloria Estefan. She was hardly a little girl born with a silver spoon in her mouth. She was born Gloria María Fajardo in Havana, Cuba, on September 1, 1957, the daughter of Gloria and José Manuel Fajardo. The Fajardos did not remain on the island of Gloria's birth for long, however. Her father was a driver and bodyguard for the Cuban president, Fulgencio Batista, and his family.

A group of socialist revolutionaries led by Fidel Castro successfully overthrew the Bastista government in 1959, before Gloria was two years old. Gloria's parents were forced to leave Cuba—Havana was no longer a safe place for the former president's bodyguard and his family.

Under leader Fulgencio Batista, at right, with his wife and son, *Cuba was strongly allied with the United States.*

The Fajardo family fled via Pan Am jet across the ninety miles of ocean between Cuba and the United States, and settled in Miami, Florida. Refusing to admit the move was permanent, José purchased return tickets. Gloria still has hers. It cost just a little more than twenty dollars.

Along with many other Cubans in exile, the Fajardo family moved into a ghetto near Miami's Orange Bowl. They had been fairly well off financially in Cuba, but they faced adjustments in a new country where they had no money coming in. The family's money troubles were made worse by social problems.

"In Miami there was a lot of prejudice at the time," Gloria recalls. "It was very difficult . . . all these Hispanics coming into one place that had never had any Hispanics at all. I remember that my mom had a really tough time dealing with [the prejudice]."

The Fajardos had been in Miami for only a brief time when Gloria's father left the city to train for a secret military mission. The good news was that he was getting paid for the job. The bad news was that it was going to be very, very dangerous.

José Fajardo had joined other Cuban exiles and the U.S. Central Intelligence Agency in a move to invade Cuba and try to win back control of the country from the new leadership, which had become openly communist. "My father went off to the Bay of Pigs and left my mother a note. That was the only reason she knew. He didn't tell her where he was going." The April 1961 invasion at the Bay of Pigs, on Cuba's southwestern coast, failed. Although José survived the battle, he was captured and sent to a Cuban prison.

José finally returned to Miami a few days before Christmas 1962, when U.S. President John F. Kennedy made a deal with Cuban leader Fidel Castro. In exchange for the release of the Cuban prisoners, the United States gave Cuba millions of dollars of food and medicine.

After José returned to Miami, he enlisted in the U.S. Army, where he quickly rose to the rank of captain. In 1966, when Gloria was eight, he was sent to Vietnam.

THE BAY OF PIGS

When Fidel Castro took over Cuba's government in 1959, the new leaders began punishing former president Batista's political officials and army officers. Many people associated with the old regime fled the country. With the help of the U.S. Central Intelligence Agency (CIA), the exiles regrouped and began planning to regain control of Cuba.

The CIA, an overseas spy organization that gathers information about U.S. enemies, became involved in Cuba when Castro allied with the Soviet Union. The United States and the Soviet Union were extremely distrustful of each other, and the United States did not want the Soviets to gain a foothold in Cuba. In addition, Castro's government had seized control of U.S.-owned businesses in Cuba.

The CIA sponsored an attack—the Bay of Pigs—in an attempt to oust Fidel Castro. The CIA recruited Cuban exiles to carry out the attack and provided weapons and war supplies. The Cuban exiles, trained quickly, believed they would have the support of the U.S. Air Force. Thirteen hundred soldiers traveled by boat and landed on the beach at the Bay of Pigs on April 17, 1961.

The CIA plan assumed that the Cuban people would rise up in revolt, driving Castro from power. Instead, the invasion was a miserable failure. The exiles had no air support. As it turned out, President Kennedy had refused to send U.S. military support, and he wouldn't order in the Air Force at the last second because things were going poorly on the ground. During the short battle at the Bay of Pigs, many soldiers died. Those who survived were captured on the beach. No Cubans rose up in revolt in response to the invasion. In fact, Castro had the support of most Cubans. The invasion was poorly planned and poorly carried out on every level.

At first, the embarrassed CIA said it had had nothing to do with the invasion—that it had been entirely planned and carried out by the Cuban exiles. But the truth quickly came out when Kennedy appeared on TV and took full responsibility for the invasion. Many Cuban freedom fighters felt that the president had gone back on his word.

President Kennedy and his wife, both standing in car, *meet with members of the Bay of Pigs invading force.*

There the United States was aiding South Vietnam in its civil war against North Vietnam. With her father again at war overseas, Gloria sang songs for him into a tape recorder and mailed him the tapes. Once he wrote her back, saying, "One day, you are going to be a star."

José Fajardo's family believes he was exposed to a highly toxic herbicide called Agent Orange during his two years in Vietnam. The U.S. Army sprayed Agent Orange over the Vietnamese jungle to kill the dense foliage so enemy soldiers might be easier to see. Many of the people who came in contact with Agent Orange became sick—very sick.

Gloria's father returned home in 1968, and his family quickly realized something was wrong. He would fall for no reason. When driving, he would stop for a red light when, in fact, the light was green. Within a couple of months, he could no longer walk. José was suffering from multiple sclerosis, a crippling disease

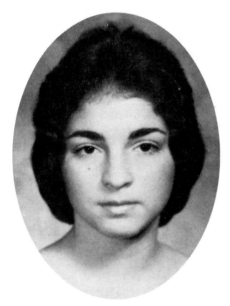

Gloria was quiet and shy when she was in high school.

that destroys parts of the brain and spinal cord. Because of his illness, he couldn't work, and Gloria's mother took a teaching job at a Miami school. Eleven-year-old Gloria had to stay home after school to take care of her ailing father, as well as her little sister Rebecca.

"I looked so much older then than I do now," Gloria said twenty years later. "I was carrying the weight of the world on my shoulders. I was used to being so full of responsibility, never being able to let go because I was afraid to. I was handling a lot, trying to be strong for my mom."

Gloria and her family spoke only Spanish in their home. She learned English in school and was an excellent student. Her smarts and good study habits always kept her at the head of her class.

As José's illness worsened, he needed constant care. "It was around the clock," Gloria remembers. "It wasn't easy. His mind went before his body. There were times when he wasn't aware of who I was, or who any of us were. It was very hard. Then it just gets to the point where you pray that the suffering will end, because you can't imagine why anyone has to go through something like that." During this time, when she was twelve, Gloria turned to music for comfort. She learned to play the guitar and spent hour after hour playing along with the radio in her room.

Gloria struggled with her father's illness and her responsibilities. She feared she would lose her mind. "I had very dark thoughts. It was a situation that had no solution. But it was good because it made me very strong. When you're a kid you think that nothing is ever going to change. . . . I thought, my God, this is going to be my life forever. But there was no other solution. We had a lady who came till three in the afternoon, but there was no one after that. My mom was working her butt off, too."

When Gloria was sixteen, José's condition worsened, and he could no longer be cared for at home. His family had to place him in a Veterans Administration hospital. Even though she no longer had to care for her father, Gloria had practically no social life in high school. She went to an all-girls' Catholic school, Our Lady of Lourdes, and was taught by nuns. Her teachers believed Gloria would join the convent and become a nun after she graduated.

In 1975, the year Gloria graduated from high school, four important things happened to change her life. First, she took a job working as a translator in the customs area of the Miami airport. Second, with her fantastic high school grades, she won a scholarship and enrolled at the University of Miami. Third, she met Emilio Estefan. And fourth, she joined his band.

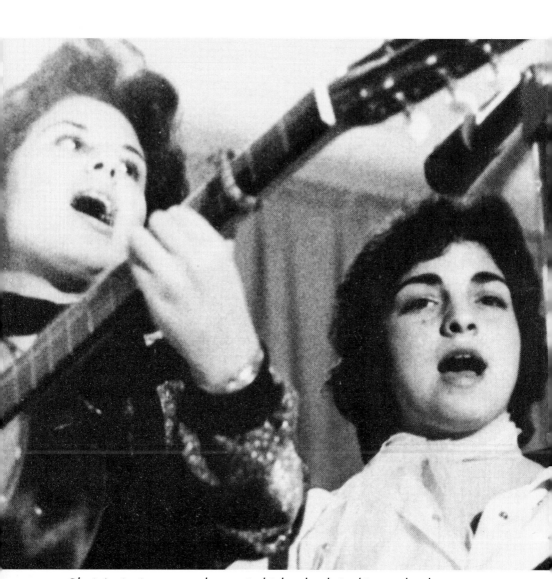

Gloria's singing career began in high school. In this yearbook photo, Gloria, right, *sings with a classmate.*

Chapter **TWO**

EMILIO

DURING THE SUMMER OF **1975,** WITH HIGH school over and college yet to start, Gloria began socializing more and making new friends. She and some friends put together a singing group, rehearsed often, and played at least one gig at a party.

The father of one of Gloria's friends knew a professional musician who agreed to give them a few tips. The musician was twenty-two-year-old Emilio Estefan, leader of a band called the Miami Latin Boys. "He came over with his accordion and these little short shorts, and I thought he was cute," Gloria recalled.

Gloria also made an impression on Emilio. "The moment when I first met her, I thought she had beautiful skin, beautiful eyes," he remembered.

After that first meeting, three months passed before they saw each other again. Gloria's mother talked her into attending a wedding, even though Gloria wasn't really interested in going. The wedding band was Emilio's Miami Latin Boys. Emilio remembered Gloria, and he asked her to join the group onstage for a couple of songs. Gloria's mother encouraged Gloria to go up and sing.

Emilio was so impressed with Gloria's singing voice that he asked her to join the band. Her first concern was whether it would affect her upcoming college studies. Gloria's mother did not like the idea of her joining an all-male band. Singing at a wedding was one thing, but at nightclubs was quite another. Gloria's mom finally gave her permission to join, but she insisted that Gloria's cousin, Mercedes "Merci" Navarro—who also sang—join, too.

Gloria told Emilio she would join his band, but she would sing only on weekends so she could keep up with her schoolwork. Emilio agreed to the conditions—and that was how Gloria began her musical career. With the addition of the young women to the group, the Miami Latin Boys needed a name change. The Miami Sound Machine was born.

During Gloria's first days as a professional singer, she and Merci did backup vocals. It never occurred to Gloria that someday she would be in the spotlight. If she had thought about singing the lead, she would have been terrified. Gloria found that the most difficult part of being in a band, for her, was overcoming her shyness.

"I didn't want to be a performer," she said years later. "When I was singing, I always stared at the floor. Performing wasn't enjoyable for me. What I loved most about the band when I joined was the rehearsals, putting the music together, writing, recording. The performance part was something I did because I had to. And I was so secure being behind the guys. When they started pushing me out in front, it was hard. It was kind of baptism by fire there. The first time I had to sing apart from the band, it was just me and the soloist, and the rest of the band was about fifty feet behind me. I was like aargh! My umbilical cord. But it makes you grow, you know."

It took time for Gloria to overcome her stage fright. Here she performs with the Miami Sound Machine in 1987.

Eventually, Gloria grew more comfortable being the lead singer. "Just growing into the sheer enjoyment of what I do has taken time," she said. "I just try to do more of what I did in the living room of my house. And that's the whole idea, approaching it in that way."

The "living room" method was Emilio's idea. During her time of painful stage fright, Emilio always told Gloria to act on stage the same way she acted when she was with him. He also thought she could become a top-notch performer. He would tell her she could improve herself ninety-five percent. "Emilio saw a side of me that I didn't let people see," Gloria says. "He was trying to make me confident, but at the time I could've smacked him. People mistook my shyness for being stuck up. A performer can't afford to be shy."

Gloria's early insecurity was not helped by the glares she got from some disapproving people in the audience. Salsa music had almost always been performed by men. Gloria tried not to be bothered by those who thought a woman should not be on stage. She had been brought up to disregard social limitations on what a woman could and couldn't do. Gloria ignored the criticism.

"I came from very strong women role models, my mother and my grandmother," Gloria said. "My mother always taught you can do anything you want, and there was never any talk of, well, you are a woman and you can't do this. On the contrary, they were wonderful role models for me in that way."

CELIA CRUZ: QUEEN OF SALSA

elia Cruz, the "Queen of Salsa," has been Gloria's idol ever since Gloria was little. Cruz, famous for her catchy Afro-Cuban rhythms, was born in Havana, Cuba, probably during the 1920s; she doesn't reveal the year of her birth.

When Celia was little, both she and her parents wanted her to be a teacher when she grew up. But she was a talented singer. As a girl, one story is told, Celia sang lullabies to smaller children at home, and her voice was so pretty that the neighbors would come over to listen. When Celia decided to pursue a singing career, her parents insisted that she be chaperoned at all her performances. The chaperones were older women from the family.

Celia sang on Cuban radio programs during the 1940s. She studied at Havana's Conservatory of Music from 1947 to 1950. In 1950, she was hired as lead singer for the island's top dance band, La Sonora Matancera. She soon made her first recordings.

Celia and the band left Cuba not long before Fidel Castro took over. After a short period in Mexico, the band—with whom Celia remained until 1965—settled in the United States. In 1966, Celia joined the orchestra of Tito Puente.

In 1973, Celia sang a role in *Hommy*—a Latin Opera by Larry Harlow—in Carnegie Hall. In 1982, she had a reunion with La Sonora Matancera. The National Ethnic Coalition of Organizations gave her the Ellis Island Medal of Honor (Mayor's Liberty Award) in 1986. Through her career, she has released seventy-four albums. She has been honored at special concerts, including sold-out performances at Madison Square Garden in New York on her birthday. She is known for her gaudy costumes as well as her musical skills. Castro, however, has never forgiven Celia for deserting her native island, and his government has refused to allow her to reenter Cuba—even to see her parents near the end of their lives.

Some people have said the Miami Sound Machine was a traditional salsa band that turned into a pop band, but Emilio viewed the band's evolution differently. Making Gloria part of the band was part of a point Emilio wanted to make—that the historical traditions of Cuban music, based in Cuba, no longer applied. The band members were Cuban, yet they were also American. They were Miami.

Despite Emilio and Gloria's initial attraction to each other, months passed before Emilio asked Gloria out. He later explained that he had too much respect for

Gloria has fun during a photo shoot with Miami Sound Machine band members.

Gloria and her past to try to start a romance with her too quickly. "Love is something that grows, and I remember telling my mother, 'I am not going to make a move on this girl unless I am serious. She's been through too much,'" he said.

Before too long, Emilio had become serious. On the Fourth of July in 1976, with the United States celebrating its bicentennial, Emilio kissed Gloria for the first time. Then he started telling Gloria how well he thought they would get along if they got married.

Emilio formally proposed in February 1978. That spring, Gloria graduated from the University of Miami, having earned her degree in psychology and communications. She and Emilio were free to make wedding plans.

On September 2, 1978, the day after her twenty-first birthday, Gloria married Emilio in Miami. The wedding took place on a rainy day, and Gloria walked down the aisle alone. She did not want anyone to stand in for her father, who was still very ill in the veterans hospital. Immediately following the ceremony, Emilio and Gloria and the rest of the wedding party went to the hospital to see José.

Gloria was very tense. José was so sick that Gloria wasn't sure he would understand why she and the others had come. He sometimes didn't recognize his family. But when José looked at the bride and said, "Glorita" (Little Gloria), the marriage was somehow made official.

Once Gloria became comfortable with having an audience, she became passionate about singing on stage.

Chapter **THREE**

THE DEEJAY
TOOK A CHANCE!

IN **1977,** THE **MIAMI SOUND MACHINE RECORDED** its first album, *Renacer* (Live Again), on a budget of two thousand dollars. The album came out on a local Miami record label.

The band members for *Renacer* were Juan Marcos Avila on bass, Kiki Garcia on drums, Raul Murciano on keyboards and saxophone, Emilio on percussion, and Gloria and Merci performing vocals. Most of the songs were in Spanish, but Emilio insisted on including some songs with English lyrics as well. Even in the earliest days of the Miami Sound Machine, when Latin music lovers made up the band's fan base, Emilio positioned the group to reach a broader audience.

WHO'S WHO IN THE BAND

There have been hundreds of musicians who have backed up Gloria Estefan during her career, from the earliest days of the Miami Sound Machine to the present. Some of the more noteworthy band members are:

Allen, Donna backup vocalist on *Hold Me, Thrill Me, Kiss Me; Destiny,* and *gloria!*

Anderson, Kenny tenor, alto, baritone, and soprano saxophones, as well as flute. Joined in April 1996.

Avila, Juan Marcos bassist, original member. Left the Miami Sound Machine in 1985.

Barlow, Randy trumpet player, songwriter. Joined in August 1985. Has also worked as a backup musician for Jon Secada. Writes songs and produces records for the Estefans' production company.

Calle, Ed guest saxophonist.

Casas, Jorge bassist, songwriter. Joined in 1987.

Cortez, Betty keyboards, backup singer.

DeFaria, John guitarist, songwriter. Joined in 1987.

Enrique, Luis percussionist on *Abriendo Puertas* and *Mi Tierra.*

Estefan, Emilio percussionist, founder of the band. Retired as a musician in 1982 but remained as band's manager, producer, and songwriter. Married Gloria in 1978.

Estefan, Gloria lead vocalist, composer of most ballads, sole remaining original member.

Garcia, Kiki percussionist, original member, composer of "Dr. Beat," and "Conga." Once considered the "engine" of the band. Left the Miami Sound Machine in 1988.

Mitchell, Tim lead guitarist on *Mi Tierra* and the Evolution tour.

Mulet, Teddy brass player. Joined in 1986. Also did backup vocals on *Mi Tierra*. Born in Puerto Rico.

Murciano, Mercedes "Merci" Navarro vocalist, original member. Left band in 1982. Cousin of Gloria.

Murciano, Raul keyboards, saxophone, original member. Left band in 1982.

Ostwald, Clay keyboardist, songwriter. Joined in 1987.

Padilla, Rafael percussionist. Joined in 1985.

Quiñones, Cheito brass player, backup vocals. Childhood friend of Teddy Mulet from Puerto Rico.

Scaglione, Mike "Scaggs" saxophone. Joined in 1987.

Secada, Jon backup vocals, songwriter during early 1990s before his solo career took off.

Wright, Betty backup vocalist. Formerly Gloria's vocal coach.

Wright, Wesley B. guitarist. Joined in 1980, left the Miami Sound Machine in 1985.

Poverty is one of Cuba's biggest problems.

The band released two more albums in the next two years—*Miami Sound Machine* in 1978 and *Imported* in 1979. The title of the latter album referred to the members of the band, who had been "imported" to the United States from Cuba.

In 1979, Gloria and Emilio returned to Cuba to help Emilio's brother José and his kids leave Cuba for the United States. "We were able to get Emilio's brother a visa through Costa Rica because we were friends with the president [of Costa Rica]," Gloria said. "When my brother-in-law announced that he was going to leave the country, they made things very, very difficult for him and his kids—so we went."

Gloria found the conditions in her homeland appalling. "People are suffering there. One of the things that I like most is a hot shower, but in Cuba maybe three drops would come out. You had to wait for water. There was no hot water. A mother can't bathe her baby."

Back in the United States, Emilio and the band continued to reach for success. There was no way the Miami Sound Machine was going to make much money selling independently produced albums without a large fan base, so the band used the records to generate some interest. Every disc jockey in every Miami nightclub received a free album.

The deejays played the songs, and before long, the Miami Sound Machine was Miami's favorite dance band. The band's local success grew so much that a record company came calling. In 1980, Discos CBS International signed the Miami Sound Machine to record Spanish-language albums for its worldwide Latin markets. As a result, the Miami Sound Machine became well known in Central and South America during the early 1980s. The band's albums hit the top of the charts in Venezuela, Peru, Panama, and Honduras.

About the same time, the Estefans experienced great sorrow and great joy in their personal lives. Gloria's father, after twelve long years of illness, passed away. The Estefans also had their first child. Their son, Nayib, was born on September 2, 1980.

These profound personal events barely slowed work for the band. The Miami Sound Machine recorded four albums with Discos CBS International over the next four years, between 1980 and 1984. The albums were *MSM*, *Otra Vez* (Another Time), *Río* (River), and *A Toda Máquina* (At Full Speed). Before the record deal, the band had been used to playing "big" shows in Miami, in which they would sell out arenas of twenty-five hundred seats. Touring Latin America to promote the new records, the Miami Sound Machine found itself selling out soccer stadiums and playing in front of thirty to forty *thousand* people. When the band's contract with Discos CBS International ran out, it almost immediately signed another, bigger contract with Epic Records, another division of CBS.

As the band became more popular, problems arose among its members. Gloria's cousin Merci, who had joined the band with Gloria, had married Raul Murciano, the keyboard and saxophone player. Raul was bitter that the Estefans were in absolute control of the band. During a big argument, Emilio told Raul he was free to leave if he didn't like how the band was operated. Raul left, quitting the band in 1982 and taking Merci with him.

That same year, Emilio retired as a performer. Instead of performing with the band, he stayed offstage with Nayib while Gloria was onstage. Emilio also quit his day job at Bacardi Imports to manage the band full-time. At Bacardi, he had been doing very well as director of Hispanic marketing—earning one hundred thousand dollars a year by the time he quit.

Gloria and Emilio knew how much Americans loved to dance, and they knew how much fun it was to dance to Latin music. But most Americans liked only English-language songs. The Estefans knew that if the Miami Sound Machine was ever going to be popular in the United States, the band would have to write and record most of its songs in English. But they still had to persuade the record company.

In 1984, Epic Records allowed the Miami Sound Machine to record just one song in English. "Dr. Beat" was released as the B side of a single—that is, on the side that disc jockeys don't usually play. But after listening to "Dr. Beat," deejays played that song instead of the Spanish ballad on the A side.

Gloria recalled the first time she heard "Dr. Beat" on a local Miami radio station: "We believed in that song and didn't know they were going to play it. We were in rehearsal, and somebody came in with a radio— 'Listen!' It was 'Dr. Beat.' I go, 'Oh, my God! I can't believe this!' The deejay took a chance and played it."

The composer of "Dr. Beat" was Kiki Garcia, the wildman percussionist. His lively stage presence made him one of the band's most popular members during live gigs. Although "Dr. Beat" was just a fun disco tune with a Latin flavor, it had a gimmick that nightclub dancers found irresistible—a siren at the beginning calling all dancers onto the dance floor.

Because the song was getting airplay, Epic Records quickly reissued it, this time with an extended-play dance version on the A side of a ten-inch record. That version sold so well that it hit the Top 10 on the U.S. dance charts. The Miami Sound Machine was on its way.

Four original members of the Miami Sound Machine are, clockwise from left, *Juan Marcos Avila, Kiki Garcia, Emilio Estefan, and Gloria.*

Chapter **FOUR**

CONGA

WITH "DR. BEAT" SELLING WELL, THE EXECUTIVES at Epic Records granted Emilio's request to record an English-only album. The new record, *Eyes of Innocence,* sold well in both Europe and the United States. These markets had been out of the band's realm as long as the vocalists sang mainly in Spanish.

Encouraged by the success, Emilio signed on a trio of record producers to help the Miami Sound Machine make its next record. The trio included Rafael Vigil, Joe Galdo, and Lawrence Dermer—who were known collectively by an unflattering, but fun, professional name, The Jerks. Emilio met The Jerks while they were recording a jingle for a radio commercial. He learned that they had been recording Latin music

Gloria dances to "Conga" at a concert in Tokyo in 1986.

for an aerobics exercise video. When he heard their music, he knew their production style—their "sound"—was what he wanted for the Miami Sound Machine.

Emilio hired The Jerks for the next Miami Sound Machine album. *Primitive Love,* released in 1985, was all English as well. Gloria and Emilio knew which song from the album they wanted to release as the first single. Called "Conga," it was much like other songs with a conga beat, with one major exception— the lyrics were in English. At Cuban parties, conga songs are a tradition. After a night of music and dancing, the evening wraps up with a conga song. When the conga starts, everyone gets up, forms a single-file line, and dances—three steps forward, followed by a kick.

Even with the Miami Sound Machine's success with "Dr. Beat," the executives at the record company did not want to release "Conga" as a single. They said it was too American for the band's Latin audience and too Latin to appeal to non-Latins. Gloria couldn't believe her ears. Hadn't the executives been paying attention? They were *still* missing the point. "We're a blend!" she said.

Eventually, the record executives agreed to release "Conga" as a single. It wasn't just a hit. It was a monster hit! The song became a regular feature at many dance clubs across the United States. It became nearly impossible to attend a wedding reception without seeing a conga line.

The single reached the Top 10 on *Billboard* magazine's "Hot 100." By the time "Conga" dropped off the charts, the Miami Sound Machine and Gloria Estefan were household names across the United States.

The song was the ultimate "crossover" hit. It was extremely popular with both Latin and non-Latin listeners, just as Gloria and Emilio had predicted. In fact, "Conga" remains the only song in history to appear on *Billboard*'s pop, soul, dance, and Latin charts at the same time. Gloria could not have been more correct when she described the band as a blend.

Not all of the Miami Sound Machine's songs were hot Latin-beat salsa numbers. The band knew how to change the pace. One of Gloria's roles was to slow things down with romantic dance songs. The band's follow-up single to "Conga" was "Words Get in the Way," which established this other side of the Miami Sound Machine—Gloria's side. She wrote vividly romantic lyrics laid over beautiful melodies with pop hooks. They had tremendous mass appeal. Nearly everyone could relate to the feelings expressed in "Words Get in the Way," a song Gloria wrote after a big argument with Emilio:

> Your heart has always been an open door
> But baby I don't even know you anymore
> And despite the fact it's hurting me
> I know the time has come to set you free.

"Words Get in the Way" went to number five on the U.S. pop charts. The third single from *Primitive Love*, "Bad Boy," a disco tune, also made the Top 10.

Of all the aspects of Gloria's show business career, she considers composing songs the most challenging. "Writing is the most difficult thing for me," she says. "It's a process. Like having a baby, it starts and it finishes. And each song is so unique and so separate. It's hard to know where I'm ever going to get the next one. But somehow it comes—through life. You keep living and you have experiences, and this or that will inspire you. Hopefully, it will keep coming."

Most artists who record songs in more than one language write the lyrics in one language and then directly translate those words into the other language, making minor adjustments so the words fit. But Gloria and her collaborators write two separate sets of lyrics, so the meaning of the song in Spanish might be quite different from the meaning in English. Then again, some songs she writes have both English and Spanish intermixed—in "Spanglish," as she likes to say.

By 1985, the spotlight at Miami Sound Machine shows fell almost exclusively on Gloria. She had

Although Gloria enjoyed singing and performing onstage, she also liked songwriting.

Cold weather doesn't stop Gloria from putting her bare feet into cement on the "Boulevard of Stars" in Amsterdam in 1985. Emilio, right, and Nayib, left, look on.

emerged as the lead singer—the star—and the band had become her backup band. Gloria had become more confident and comfortable in her role as a performer, and her voice, good looks, and energetic stage presence had captivated the band's fans. Her popularity reached beyond Latin America and the United States, into Europe as well. In the Netherlands that year, Gloria put her footprints on the Boulevard of Stars in Amsterdam—a celebrity tribute similar to the stars on Hollywood's Walk of Fame.

In 1986, the Estefans officially became a corporation. Estefan Enterprises, Inc., was formed, with Emilio as president and Gloria as vice president. Each owned half the company.

Although they had already achieved great success and had earned more money than they'd ever dreamed, their future success was not assured. The Miami Sound Machine, even after one hit album and three hit singles, hadn't settled into a predictable niche. Depending on the song, they might sell well to the Latin market, the disco market, or the pop market.

Many people in the music business still considered the success of "Conga" a fluke. It wasn't a bad song, they said, but its popularity with English-speaking people— for whom the musical style hadn't been intended— came as a surprise and wasn't a guarantee of future success. The success of two follow-up singles, the first a ballad and the second a disco tune—both of which had a more typical American pop sound and successfully sold to English speakers—helped calm record executives. Yet if the Miami Sound Machine's next album didn't sell well throughout the United States, the Estefans would be back to singing primarily in Spanish and working mostly in Miami.

Gloria, Emilio, and the band were up to the task of producing music with mass appeal. The follow-up record, released in 1987, was called *Let It Loose*, and it sold an incredible eight million copies.

Gloria's fans didn't seem to mind the band's new focus on her.

Chapter **FIVE**

SPOTLIGHT ON GLORIA

WITH THE RELEASE OF *LET IT LOOSE,* EMILIO more sharply focused the spotlight on Gloria. The band was now billed on the album cover as "Gloria Estefan and the Miami Sound Machine." The move caused some criticism from the press. *People* magazine said the new billing ruined one of the great band names and perhaps meant that Gloria's ego was getting out of control.

The public didn't seem to mind the shift. Four of the album's singles—"1, 2, 3," "Anything for You," "Rhythm Is Gonna Get You," and "Can't Stay Away from You"— were hits. No one called the group's success a fluke anymore. To promote the album, the Miami Sound Machine embarked on a twenty-month tour.

The Let It Loose tour went around the world, to Japan and other parts of Asia and to Canada. By the time the tour was over and the sales figures for the album came in, Gloria knew she did not have to worry about being called a "one-hit wonder" anymore. She had made it.

Gloria was also well past her stage fright. Instead of being too shy to perform, Gloria found she felt a letdown after performances: "When you get offstage with all these thousands of people loving you, the saddest part is to go back to your hotel room by yourself," she said.

As the album's producers, Emilio and The Jerks received a Grammy nomination for producers of the year. The nomination was a sign that record-industry experts considered the Miami Sound Machine sound to be state-of-the-art. Although Emilio and The Jerks didn't win the Grammy, the Miami Sound Machine did win an American Music Award for best pop/rock band of the year in 1988. The band had become one of the most popular in the United States.

"Conga" had inspired a rage for conga lines throughout the United States. The town of Burlington, Vermont, had won an entry in the *Guinness Book of World Records* for creating the world's longest conga line with about eleven thousand dancers participating. Folks in Miami didn't think it was right that the Guinness record belonged to out-of-towners, so they asked Gloria to organize an effort to break Burlington's record. Organizers planned for the Miami conga line to be formed at the 1988 Calle Ocho (Eighth Street) Festival in Miami, where Gloria and the band were scheduled to perform anyway.

The Calle Ocho Festival, named after one of the main boulevards running through Miami's "Little Havana" neighborhood (an area where many Cubans live), is held during the first two weeks of March. It started in the mid-1970s as little more than a neighborhood street fair, but it grew in popularity along with the Miami Sound Machine.

For the 1988 festival, Gloria turned to the local newspapers and TV stations to get the word out, and people showed up. As the conga line formed, Gloria cheered and sang from atop a stand overlooking Calle Ocho. No one could see from one end of the line to the other—it seemed to go on forever. At its longest, the conga line stretched three miles through the streets of Miami. When the dancers were counted, nearly 120,000 people had joined the line to claim the Guinness record.

With the band's continuing success—and the long, grueling tour—came more problems related to the amount of control Emilio and Gloria had over the band's direction and business. More musicians quit. Most notable among the departures was Kiki Garcia, who had written "Dr. Beat" and "Conga." The Jerks had also moved on. Except for the Estefans, all the other band members who had formed the original Miami Sound Machine were gone.

There were new band members: Clay Ostwald, who played keyboard, wrote songs, and helped produce records; Jorge Casas, a songwriter and bassist; John DeFaria, a songwriter and guitarist; and Randy Barlow, a songwriter and trumpet player.

Gloria's next album, released in 1989, was titled *Cuts Both Ways*. Fans noticed a striking difference immediately. The band's name, Miami Sound Machine, appeared nowhere on the cover. Gloria Estefan received sole billing and has ever since.

Of the ten songs on *Cuts Both Ways,* seven were composed by Gloria. The first single, a Gloria ballad called "Don't Wanna Lose You," went to number one.

Gloria poses for backstage photos after receiving her 1989 American Music Award.

The international music agency BMI recognized Gloria as 1989 songwriter of the year. For the first time, Gloria's songwriting skills were being recognized by the music industry.

As with the previous album, Emilio planned a promotional tour. But this tour was shorter to allow nine-year-old Nayib to accompany his mother and father. The band went to Europe for the first time and sold out three nights in England.

After the tour in Europe, Gloria was scheduled for a series of concerts in the United States, including one in New York City's Madison Square Garden. But those shows had to be postponed and rescheduled when Gloria returned from Europe with the flu. Her coughing bouts ruptured a blood vessel in her throat, and her doctor advised her to stop singing for two months.

In January 1990, Gloria performed at the American Music Awards and the Grammy Awards. In early March, Gloria received the Crystal Globe Award from CBS because of her excellent album sales. From there, Gloria and the band went about completing the tour, making up the shows that had been postponed when Gloria was ill. But not all of the shows were destined to be performed.

*In early 1990, Gloria, Emilio, and their son Nayib meet with
President George Bush,* left, *in the White House.*

Chapter **SIX**

THE ACCIDENT

BAD THINGS HAPPEN SOMETIMES, WITH NO WARNING
at all. That is the way it was for Gloria on the morning of March 20, 1990. Just the day before, Gloria,
Emilio, and Nayib had met with President George
Bush at the White House in Washington, D.C. President Bush and Gloria had talked about Gloria's recent
antidrug campaign. Afterward, the family took a tour
bus to New York to have dinner with Latin singer
Julio Iglesias. They told him that things couldn't be
going better for them. Gloria's upcoming shows were
all sellouts; tickets were so hard to get that scalpers
were asking huge prices for them.

The next morning, March 20, the Estefans boarded
their bus and headed northwest. They were traveling

by bus from New York City to Syracuse, New York, where she was scheduled to perform that night. The tour bus had been designed to be as comfortable as a bus could be. Resembling a long, skinny dormitory, it had room for twelve people to sleep. There were three color TVs, each with a VCR. A refrigerator was filled with food and beverages.

The trip to Syracuse was a five-hour ride through the mountainous terrain of eastern Pennsylvania and upstate New York. Emilio sat at the front of the bus and made business calls on his cellular phone. In order to keep up with his schoolwork, Nayib worked with a tutor at the back of the bus. Gloria curled up on a couch and fell asleep watching TV. Seventeen miles south of Scranton, Pennsylvania, on Interstate 380, an accident occurred just ahead of the Estefan tour bus. The roads were slippery because of a late-winter snowstorm, and a tractor-trailer rig had jack-knifed. The accident was completely blocking the highway and the Estefan bus was forced to stop until the road could be cleared.

Gloria woke up when the bus stopped. She looked out the window and noticed that snow was falling. She thought about how peaceful it was, how quiet. The wait probably wouldn't be long. A tow truck was already on the scene.

On the same road, behind Gloria's bus, was a semi-trailer truck filled with nineteen tons of pitted figs. Horrified eyewitnesses in the cars that had already

The tractor-trailer rig, right, *did considerable damage to Gloria's tour bus,* left.

pulled off the road saw the truck's driver, Heraldo Samuels, shift from the right lane to the left and then back again, trying to get past the traffic jam ahead. It looked as if something was wrong with Samuels's brakes, since he couldn't stop his truck.

The right front end of Samuels's truck smashed into the back of Gloria's bus. At the point of impact, there was a deafening explosion of shredding metal and shattering glass. The front of the Estefan bus smashed into the jackknifed tractor-trailer rig that was blocking the road, and for a moment, was sandwiched between the two huge trucks. The force of the crash threw Gloria off her couch. She landed on the floor and was unable to move, in incredible pain, and terrified.

Nayib had also been thrown to the floor of the bus. At first, Emilio couldn't find him because of all the debris that had fallen on top of the boy. Emilio himself had a deep cut on his hand, and he left bloody handprints as he crawled the length of the bus to get to his wife and son. He crawled through everything that had landed on the floor—videos, books, sneakers, and Teenage Mutant Ninja Turtles. When Emilio reached Nayib, he saw that the boy's shoulder was hurt. Gloria was in worse shape. She recalled the scene on the bus: "I told Emilio I broke my back, but he tried to reassure me. 'No, baby, maybe you just pulled a muscle.' But I could feel it. I remember thinking I would rather die than be paralyzed. But I told myself, 'No way. I'm not accepting this.'"

She waited, motionless, for help to arrive. "I lay flat on my back, holding Nayib's hand, staring at a point in the ceiling. In the back of my mind I couldn't escape the thought: I don't care about money. I don't care about anything except health. It is the only thing I want."

When the paramedics arrived, they strapped Gloria onto a backboard with her head held securely in place. They made sure her spine could not move. They didn't know how badly she was injured, and they didn't want to do anything that might make it worse.

"The pain was almost unbearable as I was strapped to a board and carried through a hole that used to be the windshield [of the bus]," Gloria recalls. "I could feel the snow on my face and the people looking down at me with fear in their eyes."

Yet she did not scream, and she did not panic. Thinking of her son, she held the pain in. "I was forced to really keep a lot of control, because I didn't want Nayib freaking out. There was chaos on that bus. And I still remember as a child that if you were to see your parents lose control in any situation, it would really be a very traumatic thing, because you always think that grown-ups have a grip on everything. And I didn't want him to feel that we had lost that grip for him, so he helped me hang on."

Paramedics placed Gloria in an ambulance, which took her to the nearest hospital, Community Medical Center in Scranton, forty-five minutes away. Because doctors had to determine how much nerve and spinal damage Gloria had sustained, they had to find out which parts of her body she could and couldn't feel.

Until those tests were done, Gloria could not receive any painkillers. She suffered greatly. "Believe me, I would rather give birth to ten kids in a row than go through that kind of pain again," she said. Still, Gloria told herself that the pain was a good thing, a good sign. She figured if she were paralyzed, she would not be able to feel anything at all.

At the hospital, X rays verified what doctors, and Gloria, had feared. Her back was broken. Emilio fainted when he heard the news. He quickly recovered, though, and made arrangements for Gloria's family members to be told about the accident. He wanted to make sure that Gloria's close relatives did not get the information from TV.

In the meantime, Nayib and Emilio received treatment for their injuries. Nayib had broken his collarbone. Because of his concern for Gloria and Nayib, Emilio initially refused a complete medical exam. He would learn a week later that he had also cracked a rib and separated his shoulder.

Two aides aboard the tour bus also suffered injuries. Doctors at a nearby hospital treated Lori Rooney for broken ribs and released her. Barbara Arencibia was hospitalized with a less severe back injury. The tour bus driver, Ron Jones, sustained minor cuts and bruises. Heraldo Samuels, the driver of the out-of-control truck, was also treated for cuts and bruises. Police charged him with driving a vehicle at an unsafe speed.

While Gloria was in the hospital, arrangements were made for Emilio and Nayib to sleep at a nearby Ronald McDonald House—a facility where the immediate family of out-of-town patients may stay. To help them avoid the many reporters, a hospital employee drove Emilio and Nayib back and forth.

Doctors at the Scranton hospital helped Emilio find the best possible surgeon—Dr. Michael Neuwirth of the Orthopedic Institute Hospital for Joint Diseases in New York City—to operate on Gloria. Dr. Neuwirth had performed the same operation many times before.

On March 21, the day after the crash, Gloria was placed aboard a medical evacuation helicopter for the flight to New York, where she would have the operation. During the flight, Emilio was thrilled by the sight of the sun emerging from behind a cloud. He pulled a piece of paper from his pocket and wrote down the words "coming out of the dark." Those words would carry him through his wife's ordeal and, later, inspire a hit song.

Paramedics immobilize Gloria and transport her to New York for the operation.

Waiting for Gloria at the hospital were her tearful mother and legendary salsa singer Celia Cruz, whom Gloria considered a personal hero. While she was in the hospital, Gloria received thousands of letters and gifts from concerned fans. Millions more around the world prayed for her. She received so many phone calls that a Miami media organization set up a special phone line to handle the well-wishers. More than four thousand orders of flowers arrived at the hospital for Gloria. She kept a few bouquets to brighten her room and gave the rest to other patients.

Gloria spent two weeks at the New York hospital. When she was discharged, she was wheeled into a press conference in a wheelchair. There, she astounded the press by standing up. She promised she would be as good as new in a matter of a few months. Gloria was not about to let the accident get the best of her. "About a week after it happened," she recalled, "I said to myself: 'Enough of this [feeling sorry for yourself]! You can't let life just land on you. Bad things happen of course, but you have to take control of your life.'"

A Most Delicate Procedure

Less than forty-eight hours after the March 20 snowy accident in the mountains of Pennsylvania, Gloria was in surgery at the Orthopedic Institute Hospital for Joint Diseases in New York City. During the hours before the operation, Dr. Michael Neuwirth briefed the press on the surgery, assuring them that, although the operation was delicate, he had done more than two hundred of them and considered the procedure routine. Neuwirth acknowledged that any error in the operation could result in permanent nerve damage or partial paralysis for Gloria. But, he said, there wouldn't be any errors.

In the operating room, a fourteen-inch incision was made down the center of Gloria's back to give Dr. Neuwirth access to the damaged portion of Gloria's backbone. He took a piece of bone from Gloria's hip—a bone graft—and used it to help repair the broken bone in Gloria's back. Neuwirth repositioned the broken vertebrae that had been pressing on Gloria's spinal cord and causing her such extreme pain. Almost immediately, operating-room personnel could see an improvement in the nerve function of Gloria's legs.

While Dr. Neuwirth was operating, he discovered a herniated (pushed out of its normal position) disc, a condition totally unrelated to the accident, which he fixed as well. All the vertebrae were realigned—moved back into their proper position. Then precautions were taken to keep them from slipping out of place.

Two slender metal rods made out of titanium were placed alongside Gloria's spine, one on each side. These rods would act like a permanent splint to keep her backbone straight. Each rod was attached to her vertebrae by eight tiny hooks. A plastic surgeon closed the incision with four hundred stitches. From the first cut to the last stitch, the procedure took over three hours.

Emilio, in dark glasses, *expresses his thanks to Dr. Neuwirth for helping Gloria's recovery.*

Gloria went by limousine from the hospital to the airport. There she boarded a private jet, lent to the Estefans by Julio Iglesias, to fly home to Miami. While on the jet, Gloria built up her courage to take her first look at the scar. When she saw it, she muttered a curse and then shrugged.

At the Miami airport, a crowd of Gloria's fans had gathered. When the plane landed, Gloria insisted on walking down the stairs. Holding tightly to Emilio's arm and sometimes wincing in pain, she walked down to the runway. The crowd cheered. "I want you to know that I've felt every one of your prayers from the first moment," she told the crowd. "I hope I don't ring all the time now when I go through those things [metal detectors] at the airport," she joked.

From there, she took a limousine home, where her months-long rehabilitation began. Gloria does not talk publicly about the painful exercises she had to do to recover from her accident. Emilio remembers the first few days were so painful that Gloria would cry during her walking exercises. Gloria tried humor to combat the pain. Making a joke about the metal rods in her back, she quipped, "How do you pick up Gloria Estefan? With a magnet!"

After the accident, and even during the painful rehabilitation process, Gloria felt relief. "I'm more relaxed now," she said in an interview not long after the accident. "I was always thinking that things were going too well. Something was going to happen. And now it has. I figure I'm good now for another few years. When I think of what could have happened, I feel better—and luckier—every day."

In September 1990, Gloria made her first post-accident public appearance in a video clip she sent to the Jerry Lewis Telethon. In the clip, Gloria urged

To the surprise of reporters, Gloria stands up during her press conference before leaving the hospital.

viewers to send money to fight muscular dystrophy—a crippling disease similar to the one that killed her father. She also took the opportunity to thank all of her fans for their gifts and prayers. She did not sing on the clip, but she assured viewers that she would be back on stage soon.

Even as Gloria continued her painful recovery, she, Emilio, and their musicians were busy in the studio. They were putting together Gloria's next album, *Into the Light*. One of the featured songs was "Coming out of the Dark," cowritten by Gloria, Emilio, and Jon Secada. The song celebrated the love that carries people through tough times:

> I know the love that saved me
> You're sharing with me
> Starting again is part of the plan
> And I'll be so much stronger holding
>   your hand.

This project was special because of all Gloria had been through. She was emotional about the music and she knew her audience would be, too. "I wanted this album to be a very freeing experience for me," Gloria said, not long after the record came out. "I wanted my vocal performances to be much more emotional, and I think they are. The emotions are right there on the surface. I was very happy when I started singing again, and I wanted to share that feeling."

Soon after the record came out, doctors gave Gloria the OK for concert performances, as long as she didn't "do crazy things, like backflips off the stage." Her first live appearance on TV came within a year of her accident, as a presenter at the American Music Awards in January 1991. On March 1, 1991, Gloria was back on stage—on tour, promoting the new album.

Her first concert was on home turf, before twelve thousand screaming fans at the Miami Arena. Just before going on stage, Gloria said, "The reason this is going to be difficult is because it's going to be a first: the first time I perform this show. It is going to be a very emotional night for me."

Gloria was on stage for mere seconds before fans began weeping with joy. Their beloved Gloria was singing and dancing again before their eyes. On stage, Gloria told the crowd, "I love you, Miami. I am at a loss for words right now. I thought I had a million things to say when I got up here, but it's so hard. No matter what I say, it's not enough for all the love you've given me this year."

The accident and recovery changed Gloria forever. The experience has mellowed her, she says. "It's hard to get me in an uproar about anything, because most things have little significance compared with what I almost lost," she said.

Gloria is convinced that, without the love of her family and fans, she never would have recovered enough to resume her concerts. "The power of love inspires me and keeps me going," she said. "Love is a constant source of inspiration, surprise, and wonderment."

From Florida, the Into the Light tour traveled across the Atlantic Ocean to England, where Gloria performed nine sold-out shows. After one show in London, Gloria was the guest of honor at a huge party at the city's Hard Rock Cafe. Party hosts flew in all of Gloria's favorite Cuban food from Miami for the affair, which turned into quite a social gathering—with London celebrities begging for an invitation. After England, Gloria moved on to Germany and Sweden, where Gloria-mania was also in full swing.

With Gloria's miraculous comeback from the accident, the Estefans focused on the business side of her career. They bought Crescent Moon Studios, the studio where Gloria did most of her recording. Emilio is the president of Crescent Moon, and Gloria is vice president.

Crescent Moon earned a reputation as a state-of-the-art recording studio. Some of the world's best and most famous musicians, including the Rolling Stones, Celia Cruz, Celine Dion, Madonna, the Barrio Boyz, and Quincy Jones, have made their records at Crescent Moon.

Gloria started 1992 with a bang. On January 26, she performed during halftime at the Super Bowl game

CRESCENT MOON: ON THE CUTTING EDGE

rescent Moon Studios has been a high-tech operation as long as the Estefans have owned it. Gloria's recordings are always on the cutting edge of technology. Her 1995 Christmas CD, *Christmas Through Your Eyes,* (the title song was written for Nayib and originally appeared on Gloria's greatest hits CD) was the first recording ever made using T-1 fiber optic audio link. This audio link allowed CD-quality sound to be transmitted between recording studios. The sessions for *Christmas Through Your Eyes* were held with producer Phil Ramone in a studio in New York, the band in Los Angeles, and Gloria in Miami at her own Crescent Moon Studios.

Gloria once again used the T-1 fiber optic audio link technique in September 1997 when she recorded her portion of a new version of Leonard Bernstein's *West Side Story,* featuring various artists and produced by Dave Grusin. As was the case with her Christmas CD, Gloria didn't have to leave Miami while the band played in New York. Gloria sang the song "Tonight."

between the Washington Redskins and the Buffalo Bills. With 63,130 people watching live at the Hubert H. Humphrey Metrodome in Minneapolis, Minnesota, and some one billion more watching on TV around the world, Gloria entered the arena through dry-ice smoke, wearing strings of pearls over a black dress. For her performance, she sang "Live for Loving You" and "Get on Your Feet" from a large stage in the center of the football field.

The halftime show also featured a full symphony orchestra and thirteen hundred extras singing and dancing in a salute to the upcoming Winter Olympics. But, according to next day's papers, Gloria had stolen the show. Football crowds usually use the halftime show as a good excuse to get a hot dog. But Gloria had the crowd staying put, focusing on her, and clapping along.

Later that year, the Estefans made one of their most famous investments, and it had little to do with show business. They bought the Cardozo Hotel in the South Beach section of Miami Beach. Some have guessed that they paid as much as five million dollars for the hotel, which was built in a very distinctive, elegant style known as art deco. Under the Estefans' management, the hotel quickly became a very popular place. The hotel features a veranda restaurant called Larios on the Beach, where people can eat and look out over the waterfront. Larios won the admiration of food critics, who called it the best Cuban-American restaurant in the United States.

Once again, Emilio and Gloria fused their business acumen and Cuban heritage to create a successful endeavor. Their lives had returned to a state of normalcy as they created music and conducted business. Before long, the Estefans showed the world yet another side of themselves: their charitable side.

Residents of Miami retrieve whatever they can from their damaged homes after Hurricane Andrew leveled their neighborhood.

Chapter **SEVEN**

IT WAS LIKE THEY DROPPED A BOMB

IN AUGUST 1992, HURRICANE ANDREW STRUCK southern Florida. With winds measured at 164 miles per hour, one of the strongest storms in recorded history, the hurricane left an incredible path of destruction in its wake. While Miami was hit hard by the storm, the city's southern suburbs—an area of poorly built houses and trailer homes—sustained the worst damage. While early-warning systems kept human casualties to a minimum, people who had fled their homes returned not only unable to find their homes, but unable even to find the streets where their houses had been. Some three hundred thousand people were left homeless.

The Estefans were in Miami during the hurricane. They waited out the storm in their recording studio, huddled together. "A couple of times we peered out from the lobby," Gloria remembered, "and the sound was so horrendous that we couldn't bear that, and we stayed in. . . . At one point, at about three in the morning, the whole building got sucked to one side, and my back got plastered against the couch. I thought, here we go."

A short time later, during the Labor Day weekend, the U.S. Army invited Gloria and Emilio to visit Homestead, Florida, where the worst of the hurricane damage had occurred. Estimates were that up to

At her recording studio, Gloria sorted through toys for the victims of Hurricane Andrew.

ninety percent of Homestead had been leveled by the storm. The army wanted Gloria and Emilio to greet residents as part of an effort to cheer up the hurricane victims. The Estefans were shocked by what they saw when they arrived. "I was thinking, 'I've never seen anything like this in my life, and I hope never to see it again,'" Gloria said. "It was almost like they dropped a bomb, what I imagine people feel like in a war-torn city."

Gloria and Emilio knew that they would have to do more to help than just shake hands and tell victims how sorry they were. They decided to organize a benefit concert. They would invite some of their talented friends to perform, and all the proceeds would go to the hurricane relief fund.

The Robbies—a prominent family in Miami—gave the Estefans free use of Joe Robbie Stadium, the home of the Miami Dolphins football team, for the concert. Among the stars who agreed to perform were the Bee Gees, Paul Simon, Whoopi Goldberg, Jimmy Buffett, Ziggy Marley, Ruben Blades, and Crosby, Stills, and Nash.

The concert was held on September 26, 1992, attracting more than fifty-three thousand people. The show turned into a huge party, with the crowd singing along and dancing until three o'clock in the morning. The concert raised more than four million dollars— but Gloria was not through. She had written a song, "Always Tomorrow," which became the unofficial theme song for the hurricane relief effort. Its message brought hope to millions of Floridians affected by the disaster:

'Cause there's always tomorrow
To start over again
Things will never stay the same
The only one sure thing is change
That's why there's always tomorrow.

"Always Tomorrow," written by Gloria Estefan. Copyright 1992. Foreign Imported Productions & Publishing, Inc. (BMI). International rights secured. All rights reserved.

And then Gloria did even more. She released a video of the song that included an address where viewers could send money to help hurricane victims.

Gloria received several awards for her charity work. She once again caught the attention of U.S. President George Bush, who was impressed with her relief work. President Bush asked Gloria to become a member of the U.S. delegation to the United Nations. Gloria gratefully accepted the position, adding another title to her résumé: Gloria Estefan, Diplomat. She spent three months attending the Forty-Seventh General Assembly of the United Nations, serving on the Third Committee on Human Rights. When the United States issued statements during hearings on Cuba, Gloria was the one to make the speech. Gloria welcomed the opportunity to speak out on behalf of the people of Cuba, who she feels are oppressed by Castro's government.

Over time, Gloria had become a superstar with a built-in audience for her music—no matter what she decided to record. She had the freedom to move away from the sound that had made her successful. She could take risks.

In 1993, Gloria released a solo album called *Mi Tierra* (My Land). The compact disc (CD) was filled with old Spanish-language love songs updated in a modern recording studio. Gloria explained the concept: "We wanted to get a traditional Cuban sound, but new. That's how the idea for this selection of songs was born: themes with an old heart—as if they were recorded a long time ago, but with the freshness and technical means of today." Many listeners felt the CD captured the sound of Cuban music from the 1930s, 1940s, and 1950s—but with a 1990s point of view. The CD won the 1994 Grammy for best tropical album.

In May 1993, Gloria went to Ellis Island in New York Harbor, where immigrants were processed for entrance into the United States many years ago. There, Gloria was presented with the Ellis Island Congressional Medal of Honor—the highest award the United States gives to a citizen born outside the country. She received the award for being a positive representative of Cuban immigrants as well as a worldwide ambassador for the United States.

As a guest delegate to the United Nations, Gloria listens to a translation of a speaker.

By 1994, Gloria's life had reached new heights: she had a fantastic career and she was winning many awards. She had a star on Hollywood's Walk of Fame. Her alma mater, the University of Miami, gave her an honorary doctor of music degree. The Coalition of Hispanic American Women honored her for her achievements in the arts and entertainment field.

But there was one thing Gloria also wanted: another child. She was having difficulty becoming pregnant. A medical examination determined that the bus accident had damaged one of Gloria's fallopian tubes, which are critical for conceiving a baby. Gloria had corrective surgery, but her doctors feared a pregnancy would put too much pressure on her backbone, still held in place by titanium rods. So, even though her fallopian tube had been fixed, there was still great risk involved when Gloria became pregnant in 1994.

In the end, Emily Marie Estefan was born by cesarean section on December 5, 1994, and both mother and daughter came through the procedure with flying colors. Emily joined Emilio, Gloria, Nayib, and two Dalmatians named Lucy and Ricky in the Estefan family. Only weeks after her birth, Emily made her first public appearance, along with the rest of the Estefan family, on *The Oprah Winfrey Show*.

In September 1995, Gloria fulfilled a lifelong dream: returning to her homeland to perform. Gloria had not been to Cuba since 1979, when she went with Emilio to help his brother leave the country. Because of her

Gloria and Emilio with their infant daughter, Emily Marie

In 1995, Gloria, with Emilio, accepts her Grammy for Best Tropical Latin Performance.

strong objections to Fidel Castro, Gloria refuses to seek permission from his government to perform in Cuba. Castro does not control all of Cuba, however. A small portion of the island, Guantánamo Bay, is under the control of the United States. Cuban exiles seek refuge at the U.S. naval base on Guantánamo Bay and remain there until they are allowed to enter the United States. With the help of the U.S. Navy, Gloria arranged to spend a day at Guantánamo Bay, visiting with the sailors and exiles there and performing songs for them. She sang selections from her new CD, *Abriendo Puertas* (Opening Doors). After the show, Emilio told Gloria that her father would have been very proud of her if he had been alive.

Gloria recorded the songs on *Abriendo Puertas* in Spanish. The CD featured songs with Christmas themes, and it combined musical styles from many Latin American countries. Among the musical styles found on the CD are Cuban *son,* Colombian *cumbia, merengue, mambo, guaganco* and, of course, salsa. Gloria said that just as the musical styles of Latin countries can be joined to become one, so could the people.

Gloria decided which musical styles to include by monitoring her fan base in various Latin and South American regions, then recruiting musicians from those areas to perform on the CD. "You have to reach a certain level where you have a strong enough fan base where they will be curious about what you do, and they'll listen to it. . . . Hopefully, fans will like the direction we've moved and grown into, since all of these projects eventually become a part of you," she said.

The album did not sell as well as *Mi Tierra* had, and some critics said the musical arrangements sometimes overwhelmed Gloria rather than backing her up. The people who vote on the Grammy awards didn't find anything wrong with the CD, however. Gloria won a 1995 Grammy—her second Grammy—in the category of Best Tropical Latin Performance.

Gloria spends some leisure time in Miami on her boat.

Chapter **EIGHT**

TRAGEDY ON BISCAYNE BAY

ON SEPTEMBER 24, 1995, GLORIA AND EMILIO'S life received another dose of tragedy. The day started out beautifully. The famous couple had a rare day off, with nothing to do but enjoy themselves. They decided to spend the day cruising Miami's Biscayne Bay and the Atlantic Ocean on their thirty-foot pleasure boat. Out on the water, the Estefans were having a wonderful time, at one point pulling up alongside a tourist boat and coming so close that Gloria was able to reach over and high-five the fans.

The bay was crowded with people enjoying the day on the water. Many of them were tourists who, for sixty-five dollars an hour, could rent small, two-seat personal watercraft, commonly called wet bikes. The

Wet bikes are a popular, though dangerous, form of water recreation.

little watercraft are powerful and scoot quickly over the waves.

Since no training was required to rent the personal watercraft, there were many accidents on the bay each year. Some accidents resulted in serious injury. The wet bikes seemed like toys, and many tourists climbed aboard without knowing how dangerous they could be. The most popular and dangerous trick to perform on wet bikes is jumping wakes (the path of waves left behind a moving boat). To jump a wake, a wet bike operator crosses the water behind a larger motor boat at a point where the wake created by the larger boat is high. When the wet bike hits the wake, the small craft goes flying through the air.

Twenty-nine-year-old law student Maynard Clarke, from Washington, D.C., had rented a wet bike on Gloria and Emilio's day off. He and his girlfriend, Tisha Greene, took the wet bike onto Biscayne Bay for an afternoon of fun. At 4 P.M., Gloria and Emilio were returning to their Star Island home after their day of boating. Reconstructing events, officials think Maynard, driving the wet bike almost head-on toward the Estefan boat, had decided to jump its wake. He probably planned to turn to the side just after he had passed the boat, but he turned too soon. Instead of crossing behind the Estefan boat, he slammed into its side. Gloria and Emilio heard the thump, then immediately looked toward the sound.

The accident had knocked both passengers off the wet bike. Tisha fell away from the large boat and was not seriously hurt. But Maynard fell under the Estefans' boat and was badly cut on the shoulders and across the throat by the twin blades of the boat's propellers.

Emilio ran to the side of the boat and looked into the water which was turning red from Maynard's blood. Emilio quickly dove into the water to help. "With that much blood . . . there are a lot of shark and barracuda," Emilio said not long after the accident. "But it's someone's life and you have to help."

By the time Emilio reached Maynard, the younger man's body was already limp. While Emilio was in the water, Gloria was on the cellular phone, calling 911. Other boaters came to help. Several people worked together to get Maynard out of the water and into the Estefans' boat. Then they sped to shore to meet an ambulance. The Estefans had done everything they could to help save Maynard's life, but his injuries were too severe. He died in the ambulance before it arrived at the hospital.

When the press learned about the accident, reporters swarmed around the famous Estefans and focused their stories on them. This struck Gloria as wrong. She told the reporters they should be talking and writing about the poor young man who had lost his life, rather than writing about her.

The Estefans were deeply saddened by the accident. A few days after the tragedy, Gloria decided she should talk to the victim's mother. Gloria knew that the woman would want to know about her son's last moments. "It was the hardest thing I ever had to do in my life," Gloria said of making the phone call. "Harder than the bus accident."

When reporters asked Maynard's family about the accident, Maynard's father mentioned that Gloria had called. He described the call as "uplifting," and added, "[Gloria] was very upset and said that she had not been sleeping. She told us if there's anything she could do to help, she will."

The more Gloria thought about the accident, the more she realized something needed to be done. The man who died had had no idea what he was doing on the wet bike. And he wasn't alone. Accidents happened regularly out on the bay. Gloria decided to take action.

The best way to reduce the number of accidents, she believed, was to require all people to take a training course before they were allowed to operate a wet bike. A course could be designed to teach drivers the basics of operating the machines. For example, if Maynard had known that a wet bike cannot be steered unless the propellers are spinning, or that the machine has no brakes, he might have been more cautious around the larger boat.

On February 7, 1996, Gloria appeared before the Florida House Committee on Natural Resources to speak about what she thought should be done. She realized she was taking advantage of her stardom—since not just any citizen could march before the state leaders and testify—but she was doing it for a good cause. At the same time, Gloria knew her ideas would not be warmly welcomed by the politicians. Personal watercraft rentals brought a lot of money into the Miami area.

Gloria talks about boating safety to reporters during a news conference with Florida governor Lawton Chiles.

Restrictions on renting wet bikes might cost the state of Florida millions of dollars in lost revenue.

In her remarks to the committee, Gloria said, "I come here as a citizen of Miami Beach, a citizen of the state of Florida, and, obviously, the celebrity has a little bit to do with why I am here. We want to shine the light on this issue. We want something passed . . . that is somehow going to make our waters safe." She then related the grim statistics on injuries and fatalities among wet bike operators.

"Obviously, what a wet biker wants to do is get airborne, jump that wake at its highest, and, unfortunately, the highest peaks are closest to the boat. . . . What we need to do is educate the people [who] are renting these vehicles so that they know not only the fun that they can have, but the danger that is involved as well. I firmly believe that education is crucial for boaters and for personal watercraft."

In the end, the Florida State Senate and House voted by wide margins to adopt Gloria's proposal as law. The law requires licensing for all boaters under age sixteen and a twenty-minute wet bike operation demonstration for new renters. At the ceremony marking the signing of the bill, Gloria sang a song to the politicians who had listened to her plea.

Gloria is quick to point out that, even though a law was passed because she took action, Biscayne Bay is still not nearly as safe as it could be. She is glad that underage boaters are off the bay, but she says most of

Gloria had promised representative Jim King of Jacksonville, Florida, that she would sing to him if he helped pass a bill on boating safety. After the bill was signed into law, Gloria kept her promise.

the problems are caused by young men in their twenties who have been drinking.

In between the tragedy and her lobbying efforts, Gloria performed for Pope John Paul II in the Vatican, the papal headquarters in Rome. She was invited to be part of a celebration for the pope's fiftieth year in the priesthood. Gloria was the only pop star asked to appear, and no doubt had gotten the pope's attention because of her strong anti-Castro stance. Castro had banned religion in Cuba when he took over. For the pope, Gloria sang "Más Allá" (Beyond), from her CD *Abriendo Puertas*. A sixty-two-piece orchestra accompanied her. Gloria also spent time in the studio preparing and fine-tuning a new album that would further enhance her stature as a musician.

Gloria sings at a concert in Paris in 1996.

Chapter **NINE**

¿Como Está Mi Gente?

GLORIA'S **1996 CD,** *DESTINY,* **WAS HER FIRST** collection of original songs in English in nearly six years. The version sold in the United States was an "enhanced CD"—a compact disc with CD-ROM features. When placed in a computer's CD drive, the music CD could display an assortment of photos of Gloria, some of which were previously unavailable. It contained a studio interview in which Gloria discussed the origins of Afro-Cuban music—many of the instruments, particularly the drums, used in Cuban music originated in Africa—and how those roots affected the music on the album. It showed a discography, a list of her albums, including sound bites from the various hits. It also showed behind-the-scenes footage from a video shoot for the CD's top single, "Reach."

Discussing her new CD in media interviews, Gloria talked again about blends. The music had been a blend from the beginning. She also had come to see her audiences as a blend. Latinos and non-Latinos party and dance side-by-side at Gloria's concerts. And her live shows are a blend of elements of Latin culture, the slow middle-of-the-road ballads that Gloria preferred when she was a child, and a snippet or two of rock and roll.

"My fans who are non-Hispanic really enjoy the Latin stuff," she said soon after *Destiny* was released. "I wanted to continue in that vein and at the same time give them something in their own language. So the feelings of the songs are still very ethnic, not just Afro-Cuban, but there is also a Colombian rhythm called *curralao* that has never been done in a song written in English. It's a rhythm from the Pacific Coast of Colombia, very little used."

There was a new, emotional richness to the lyrics, which Gloria explained by saying, "I've lived a lot of things in the past few years. Everything that you live and every emotional layer comes into your writing and your singing."

The words were in English, but the music, she said, was "Afro-Cuban, Afro-Antillean, and Afro-Caribbean at the core. . . . The songs are about all the different kinds of love—physical, maternal, and spiritual. It's a different take on love in its many forms. And, of course, there are a couple of Latin party tunes. Oh yeah, we've got to have that. That's part of our sound. Part of who we are. Our band now has nineteen pieces. It has to be a big production because, in order to do the Latin stuff, . . . you need percussion all over the place. . . . No one drummer can do it. And there are no kit drums [programmed rhythm machines], either. There are no kit drums on the entire album."

The CD contains a song called "Along Came You (A Song for Emily)" with an impromptu backup vocal by Gloria's daughter, who was two years old at the time. The song is about Emily, so Gloria wanted Emily to be near while she recorded it. Gloria's good friend Madonna (Madonna's daughter, Lourdes, and Emily are playmates) had been using the studio earlier in the day and had set up many candles. Gloria had them lit and brought Emily into the studio to look at all the flickering flames.

Then Gloria sat with Emily on her lap to rehearse the song, and just as the engineer started the tape, Emily said "Happy happy." When Gloria began to sing, Emily sang along. Gloria incorporated portions of the take into the actual CD version.

Also on the *Destiny* CD was a song for all people, "Reach." Gloria included one of her most watched performances for the closing ceremonies of the Olympics in Atlanta, Georgia, on August 4, 1996. She sang "Reach" in front of a worldwide TV audience of more than one billion people. The song, written by Gloria and Diane Warren in mere minutes, is about overcoming troubled times and coming back stronger than ever—a subject which Gloria had come to know well.

> I'll go the distance this time
> Seeing more the higher I climb
> That the more I believe
> All the more that this dream will be mine
> If I could reach.

"Reach," written by Gloria Estefan and Diane Warren. Copyright 1995. Foreign Imported Productions & Publishing, Inc. (BMI) and The 1992 Diane Warren Trust dba Realsongs (ASCAP). International rights secured. All rights reserved.

"It's about starting over and getting up and moving, so yeah, I can identify very strongly with it," Gloria said not long after the Olympics. "We really wanted the song to be something that everyone could identify with. It was done as a folk song and then, because of the grandness of the Olympics, we threw on the big drums. But it is a song for every culture."

Following her performance at the Olympics, Gloria continued a world tour, the Evolution tour. In addition, Gloria made a special side trip to the Washington, D.C., area to perform "Reach" at the January 1997 inaugural ball for President Bill Clinton and Vice President Al Gore. Just days before Gloria left for the nation's capital to entertain the president, she heard that "Reach" had been nominated for a Grammy Award.

The Evolution tour played in Miami, where Gloria did a four-night stand at the Miami Arena. Her hometown fans were emotional. It was her first tour appearance there in four years, and it was apt to be her last for some time. Gloria had said she wanted to take time off after the Evolution tour so she could spend more time raising Emily.

On opening night in Miami, Gloria rode onto the stage inside a hydraulic sphere. The sphere was covered with a white cloth. Then the cloth fell away, revealing Gloria inside wearing a white mesh top and

Gloria, onstage left, *performs at the closing ceremony for the 1996 summer Olympic Games.*

sarong skirt. She began the concert with "Get on Your Feet," and the fans obeyed, putting on a light show of their own with tiny flashlights they'd been given at the door. Gloria ripped through a blistering version of "Conga," then stopped to address the crowd. "There is no place like home. *¿Como está mi gente?* (How are my people?)," she asked. The crowd's answer was louder than a jet. "We rented this place. You can dance, sing, do whatever you want. It's our party," Gloria told them.

Only a few nights before, Gloria had come down with the flu and canceled shows in Orlando and St. Petersburg, Florida. At the Miami concert, she seemed filled with good health, spending much time at the edge of the stage, where she could shake hands and accept gifts from fans. One critic wrote, "Not many pop stars can sing a torch song credibly while holding a Snoopy doll or walking a toy dog, as she did last night."

The emotional peak of the concert came when Gloria sang "Along Came You (A Song for Emily)." While she performed the song, Estefan and Fajardo family photos were projected onto a huge screen. At the end of the song, Nayib and Emily came out on stage hand in hand. There wasn't a dry eye in the house. The following night, Gloria did it all again, same time, same arena, only this performance was broadcast live on HBO. That show was later made available on video and sold as *Evolution Tour '96: Live in Miami.*

The video was the seventh featuring Gloria's singing, either as a solo artist or as a part of the Miami Sound Machine. In Gloria's career and in Gloria and Emilio's personal business holdings, they built on their previous successes. They bought property in Miami's South Beach area, continued to expand Crescent Moon, and stayed true to their Cuban roots.

In November 1997, the Estefans' newest venture, Bongo's Cuban Cafe, opened in Disney World.

Chapter **TEN**

RESTAURATEUR, DIVA, AND MOVIE STAR

LARIOS ON THE BEACH, THE ESTEFANS' HOTEL restaurant venture in Miami, became so popular that the Estefans found themselves with an opportunity to open a second restaurant—a big one—at Disney World in Orlando, Florida. The secret to the success of Larios has been the cuisine, developed by master Cuban chefs Quintin and Carmen Lario. The Larios also created the menu at the new place, Bongo's Cuban Cafe.

The restaurant opened in the "Downtown Disney's West Side" section of Disney World on November 6, 1997, with a celebrity party. Among the Latin celebrities who showed up were former Florida Marlins pitcher Livan Hernandez and Oscar-winning actress Rita Moreno.

The restaurant is huge—sixteen thousand square feet, with more than five hundred seats! It is a two-story, pineapple-shaped structure. The two levels have both indoor and outdoor dining. There's a misty waterfall and three bars, with barstools shaped like bongo drums. The restaurant was designed to look like a Cuban mansion from the 1950s. The walls all around the inside are painted with scenes of pre-Castro Cuba. A dash of Miami is thrown in for good measure. The pillars supporting the ceiling, for example, look like palm trees.

"The fifties was a happy time in Cuba, a very appealing time," says Emilio. "We specifically created Bongo's Cuban Cafe for the entire family so they may enjoy the festive Cuba that once was—and will be again."

Opening-day festivities were broadcast live over an Internet site. With traditional Afro-Cuban bongo rhythms beating away, Gloria made a spectacular entrance, dancing her way down a spiral staircase. Behind Gloria was Minnie Mouse, dressed up like 1940s movie actress and singer Carmen Miranda, with a huge hat comprised only of tropical fruit. Minnie carried Emily Estefan in her arms.

While Gloria and Emilio's new restaurant was recreating the old Cuba, changes were taking place in modern-day Cuba. Fidel Castro invited Pope John Paul II to visit. This was surprising news because Castro had banned the public practice of religion on the island for many years. The pope invited Gloria to perform for him in Cuba, but she turned down the invitation.

Emilio explained why: "We will never sing in Cuba while Fidel Castro's regime exists. The day Gloria sings in Cuba, she will do so because Cuba is free— and we trust that this will happen soon."

"My going there would have turned a beautiful spiritual thing into a political thing," Gloria said. "I would have had to have asked permission of the Cuban government to do it—and I am not about to do that. It would have been a slap in the face of my father and everything he fought for."

The pope visited Cuba in January 1998. That year, there were further indications that Castro's ban on religion was softening. He allowed Cubans to celebrate Christmas for the first time since he had taken over in 1959. Gloria retains hope that the people of Cuba will continue to regain the freedoms they enjoyed before Castro came into power.

In the meantime, Gloria continues her singing and songwriting career. Her most recent CD is called *gloria!*, with a small *g*. It was released in two versions, one for the U.S. market and one for the global market. The big difference between the two CDs is that the international version includes a disco medley that in the United States appeared with the second single. The first single, a string-laden dance anthem called "Heaven Is What I Feel," made it to number thirteen on the U.S. pop charts.

"The music is a bit retro, really," Gloria says of the CD. "We were trying to capture the feeling of the seventies. It was a very explorative and liberating time, and music was very up and positive. Since this is our last album of the millennium, I wanted it to be a celebratory and positive-feeling album." This CD also features "Touched by an Angel," another song for daughter Emily.

After struggling with record executives at the beginning of her recording career to release singles with English lyrics, Gloria now faces the exact opposite problem. She and Emilio had to push to release as a single the song "Oye" from *gloria!,* because the lyrics are in Spanish.

In recent years, rather than go on tour, Gloria has opted to participate in television performances. In April 1998, she appeared on *Divas Live!* broadcast on the VH-1 cable station. Also performing with Gloria were superstar female vocalists Aretha Franklin, Celine Dion, Mariah Carey, and Shania Twain. Money raised by the show went to help school music programs.

The producers of *Divas Live!,* who originally had the concept to bring together some of the greatest female pop singers on one show, at first feared that the divas would try too hard to outshine one another. But, as it turned out, they had nothing to worry about. The women sang beautifully together, in perfect harmony.

Gloria performed solo and then joined Dion, Twain, and special guest Carole King for a version of King's

Three of the divas, from left to right, *are Celine Dion, Gloria, and Shania Twain.*

one-time classic hit "You've Got a Friend." Gloria had a lot of fun making the show, which was taped in front of a live audience in New York, but she thought the name of the show wasn't her style.

"This diva thing is getting a little out of hand," Gloria said after her first song on the show. "If anything, I'm a divette." The show was the highest rated program in VH-1 history. The soundtrack went on to become a hit CD.

In November 1998, Gloria again performed live on national TV, giving a two-hour concert. The occasion was an episode of the A&E network's *Live by Request* program, hosted by TV meteorologist Mark McEwen. Gloria stood in front of a full orchestra and took requests for songs from people in the audience, calling in on the phone, and sending E-mail. Whoopi Goldberg was one of the phone requesters. She asked to hear "Reach," Gloria's Olympic song.

Gloria performed in a beautiful three-piece blue velvet suit. She started the show wearing all three pieces. The look was stunning, but at least one viewer didn't think it was sexy enough. During a commercial break, a stagehand brought a message to Gloria from Emilio. "My husband wants me to strip," she said—and off came the jacket.

How does Gloria stay passionate about her music after all these years? "Well, it may come with being Latin," she says. "We're passionate about everything. That's why we try not to discuss religion and politics with anyone we love. The music energizes my heart and body. That's the way it has been for me my whole life."

Gloria's music is not known for its strong political content. That's because Gloria thinks of music as fantasy, something that should be kept separate from the realities of life. "Music has always been a wonderful form of escape," she says. "In my music, I like to focus on things that are human—things that bring us together, not things that tear us apart."

Despite this philosophy, she sings on her latest album about the heartache of being unable to perform in her native Cuba. The song is "Cuba Libre" (Free Cuba), from *gloria!* Gloria does not just yearn to perform in Cuba. She wants to soak up Cuba's lifestyle. "I'd love to be able to immerse myself in my culture," she said.

"I know they play my music in Cuba," Gloria said. "I know for a fact they play *gloria!*, because a friend of mine went there and she heard 'Heaven Is What I Feel.' I think it might be a little more difficult hearing 'Cuba Libre' being played." People living in Cuba may be harassed or imprisoned for openly criticizing the government or sympathizing with opposing viewpoints.

Throughout her music career, Gloria has given so much of herself for causes she believes in that she has been called "the Mother Teresa of Miami." Since her 1990 accident, Gloria has worked to raise money to help others with spinal-cord injuries. Along with Marc Buoniconti, who was paralyzed when he broke his neck attempting to make a tackle in a college football game, Gloria is a spokesperson for a charity organization known as the Miami Project. "There's nothing separate in this world," she says. "You have a strong effect on other people in many ways."

She urges others to become volunteers—not just for her cause, but for any cause. "Pick and choose what's special to your heart," she says. "In my whole life, all I wanted to do—even as a child it was my only dream, really—was be in a position where I could help as many people as I possibly could. Some of us get on a big platform and do things in a bigger way, but it's just as important to have some charity within your own family."

Making small changes can be important too, she says. "Just think about your particular situation and what you can do. That's all you need to do. Helping others feels good. There is nothing that feels better. Nothing I could possibly buy, nothing I could possibly receive, feels better than knowing I have made a difference in somebody's life."

Gloria and Emilio have been married for more than twenty years. Gloria says they have stayed in love

Nayib, Gloria, Emilio, and Emily enjoy a limousine ride to a Planet Hollywood opening in Amsterdam.

because they fell for each other before they were successful. "We fell in love with who we were, not the trappings or the celebrity part," she says. "We continue to love each other more so because we've had difficult experiences that have made us closer."

These days, even though Gloria and Emilio are wealthy, they have not become spoiled. There remains something in their makeup that won't allow them to take their money for granted. "It's the immigrant mentality," Gloria explains. "Both of our families were very well off in Cuba. Then all of a sudden, boom, you're here. You have nothing. It's hard to get rid of that feeling."

Their children are thriving. In 1999, Nayib turned nineteen and Emily turned five. "Both are doing great," Gloria says. "My son moved out! He's in college." Having a celebrity mom isn't always easy for Nayib, though. "My son did tell me some magazine cover came out, and his friends said, 'Man, your mom is hot!' He goes, 'Don't talk like that about my mom!'"

Gloria tries not to worry about Nayib, but it's apparent she knows the dangers that exist for young people. "You have to be positive," she told *Latina* magazine. "I have a teenage son who is always out with his friends. I could surround myself with negative thoughts about what could happen to him on the roads, with all the drunken drivers—but instead I see him surrounded by angels who guide him home every time he goes out."

Gloria and Stevie Wonder perform the halftime show at Super Bowl XXXIII.

Always willing to try something new, Gloria became, in January 1999, the first guest host of *The Rosie O'Donnell Show*, which is telecast live from New York City. She used the show as a forum to poke fun at *People* magazine, which had recently published a photo of the VH-1 divas with Gloria's image cropped out. "I am shell-shocked," she said. "I guess I wasn't devoted enough to maintain my diva status."

Shortly after the appearance, Gloria again performed for a Super Bowl audience—this time on home turf. The football game, between the Denver Broncos and the Atlanta Falcons, took place at Pro Player Stadium (formerly known as Joe Robbie Stadium), the same arena where Gloria had held her Hurricane Andrew relief concert.

The twenty-minute show, as seen on TV, opened with a filmed segment. E.T., the cute extraterrestrial of movie fame, was wandering "backstage" past a television monitor. On the screen was Gloria saying, "It's gonna be a party, Miami style."

"*Hola*, Gloria," E.T. says to the screen.

Then the scene cut to a live shot of the field, where the Big Bad Voodoo Daddies started the show with a hot rendition of their song "Go, Daddy-O." Stevie Wonder then came out and sang "Sir Duke," "You Are the Sunshine of My Life," and "I Wish." During "I Wish," tap-dancing phenomenon Savion Glover joined Stevie for a duet.

Then it was Gloria's turn. Standing on top of a huge stage in a long black dress, Gloria sang "Oye" (Listen), accompanied by many dancers and percussionists. She followed up "Oye" with "Turn the Beat Around." After that, Gloria said, "The Super Bowl is hot. Miami is hot, hot, hot!" Gloria called Stevie Wonder to join her, and the two superstars sang a medley of their hits.

Because of her dynamic stage presence, striking good looks, and intuitive fan communication, Hollywood producers have been begging Gloria to make movies for years. In 1996, she had turned down the chance to be the lead in the movie *Evita*, a role which eventually went to her friend Madonna. (Gloria did make a cameo appearance in the TV movie called *Club Med* in 1986, and Emilio played a piano player in *The Specialist* in 1994.)

Gloria's first real movie role is in the 1999 movie *Music of the Heart.* Based on the 1994 documentary *Small Wonders,* the movie *Music of the Heart* is about a music school in Spanish Harlem. It was filmed entirely in New York City. Meryl Streep starred, and Wes Craven directed. (Craven directed the horror films *Nightmare on Elm Street* and *Scream.*) Streep plays music teacher Roberta Tzavaras, and Gloria plays her friend. The movie also stars Angela Bassett, Aidan Quinn, Cloris Leachman, and Kieran Culkin. There are also cameos by real-life musicians Michael Tree, Isaac Stern, Arnold Steinhardt, Itzhak Perlman, and Mark O'Connor, all playing themselves.

Gloria has been taking acting lessons for years to prepare for a career in film. "It's great fun for me to find something that's exciting and new," Gloria said. "I'm not going to quit singing, because that's who I am. But it's nice to grow and to keep moving into different things."

As she grows and moves into different things, Gloria says she'll not combat the effects of aging. "I like my face, and even as it sags, I like it. I think I would freak out if I looked in the mirror and it was not the same face looking back at me. I can handle looking older. You've got to get older," she says.

Gloria has been a successful wife, mother, singer, songwriter, diplomat, and movie star. Her very life is an inspiration, so when she offers her philosophy of life, people pay attention. "If you really have something that you believe in and that you care about, you should pursue it with hard work, with perseverance, with patience, with diligence, with balance, and definitely with a lot of love," she says. "Because anything you do with a lot of love, you can't go wrong."

SOURCES

9–10 David Shirley, *Gloria Estefan: Queen of Latin Pop* (New York: Chelsea House, 1994), 26.

10 Marc Fest, "Interview with Gloria Estefan," *Hörzu* (September 8, 1998), 118.

14 Shirley, 31.

14 Barbara J. Marvis, *Famous People of Hispanic Heritage, Volume V* (Childs, Maryland: Mitchell Lane Publishers, 1996), 15.

14–15 Michelle Genz, "Golden Girl," *Miami Herald* (May 31, 1998), Tropic Section, 10.

17 "Gloria Estefan: Intimate Portrait," Lifetime Television Network, (January 6, 1997).

17 Daisann McLane, "The Power and the Gloria," *Rolling Stone* (June 14, 1990), 74.

19 Genz.

20 Steve Morse, "Gloria Estefan Brings Her Audiences Together," *Boston Globe* (May 31, 1996), 61.

20 McLane.

20 Anthony M. DeStefano, *Gloria Estefan: The Pop Superstar from Tragedy to Triumph* (New York: Signet, 1997), 11.

23 McLane.

28 Fest.

31 Gloria Estefan, interview by Mark McEwen, *CBS This Morning*, CBS (November 4, 1998).

35 Shirley, 55.

36–37 Ibid., 15.

42 Gloria Estefan Online, <http://www.estefan.net>, n.d.

50 Steve Dougherty, "One Step at a Time," *People Weekly* (June 25, 1990), 78.

50 Gloria Estefan and Kathryn Casey, "My Miracle," *Ladies' Home Journal* (August 1990), 99.

50 Shirley, 68.

51 Genz.

53 Gloria Estefan Online.

55 DeStefano, 69.

56 Gloria Estefan Online.

56 Shirley, 73.

57–58 Music Boulevard, <http://www.musicblvd.com>, n.d.

58 Steve Dougherty, "A Year after Her Brush with Disaster, Gloria Estefan Dances out of the Dark with a New Album and World Tour," *People Weekly* (February 18, 1991), 118.

58 "Gloria Estefan: Coming out of the Dark," (Sony Music Video Enterprises, 1991).

58 Ibid.

58 Dougherty, "A Year after... Disaster...."

59 Gloria Estefan Online.

64 Leonard Pitts Jr., "Hurricane Relief," *Miami Herald* (September 25, 1992), 22G.

65 Ibid.

67 Shirley, 72.

71 Music Boulevard.

75 Peter Castro and Cindy Dampier, "Water Hazard," *People Weekly* (October 9, 1995), 65.

76 Melina Gerosa, "Gloria's Greatest Hits," *Ladies' Home Journal* (August 1996), 40.

76 Castro and Dampier.

78 Florida House of Representatives Full Committee on Natural Resources, hearing (February 7, 1996).

82 Morse.

82 Ibid.

82–83 Ibid.

84 Ibid.

86 Fernando Gonzalez, "Air Gloria! Singer to Miami: 'It's Our Party,' " *Miami Herald* (September 21, 1996), 1A.

86 Ibid.

90 Jordan Levin, "A Cuban Fantasía Mambos into Main Street," *New York Times* (November 16, 1997), Section IX, 3.

91 Cynthia Corzo, "Gloria Refuses Invitation to Sing for Pope in Cuba," *Miami Herald* (December 20, 1997), 1A.

91 Fest.

92 Ibid.

94 *CBS This Morning.*

 94 Shirley, 14.
 95 *CBS This Morning.*
 95 Fest.
 95 "Make a Difference Next Saturday," *USA Weekend*
       (October 16, 1998), 4–5.
95–96 Ibid.
 96 Ibid.
 97 *CBS This Morning.*
 97 DeStefano, 10.
 97 Ibid.
 97 LatinoLink, <http://www.latinolink.com>, n.d.
 98 Richard Johnson, "Sweet Revenge," *New York Post*
       (January 30, 1999), 8.
100 Fest.
100 Ibid.
101 Ibid.

SELECTED BIBLIOGRAPHY

Boulais, Sue. *Gloria Estefan.* Childs, Maryland: Mitchell Lane
    Publishers, 1998.
DeStefano, Anthony M. *Gloria Estefan: The Pop Superstar from
    Tragedy to Triumph.* New York: Signet, 1997.
Gonzalez, Fernando. *Gloria Estefan: Cuban-American Singing Star.*
    New York: Millbrook Press, 1993.
Marvis, Barbara J. *Famous People of Hispanic Heritage, Volume V.*
    Childs, Maryland: Mitchell Lane Publishers, 1996.
Nielson, Shelly. *Gloria Estefan: International Pop Star.*
    Minneapolis: Abdo & Daughters, 1993.

Shirley, David. *Gloria Estefan: Queen of Latin Pop*. New York: Chelsea House, 1994.

PERIODICALS

Aroca, Santiago. "Gloria Estefan Speaks Her Mind." *Exito,* October 23, 1997, <http://www.fiu.edu/~fcf/este-fanspeaks102397.html> (August 1, 1999).

Brennan, Carol. "Gloria Estefan." *Contemporary Musicians,* November 1995, <http://www.musicblvd.com/cgi-bin/tw/14940250914858158_105_215664^s&> (July 30, 1999).

Castro, Peter, and Cindy Dampier. "Water Hazard." *People Weekly,* October 9, 1995, p. 65.

Corzo, Cynthia. "Gloria Refuses Invitation to Sing for Pope in Cuba." *Miami Herald,* December 20, 1997, p. 1A.

Dougherty, Steve. "One Step at a Time." *People Weekly,* June 25, 1990, p. 78.

———. "A Year after Her Brush with Disaster, Gloria Estefan Dances out of the Dark with a New Album and World Tour." *People Weekly,* February 18, 1991, p. 118.

Estefan, Gloria. "We Must Defend Everyone's Freedom." *Miami Herald,* September 28, 1997, p. 3L.

Estefan, Gloria, and Kathryn Casey. "My Miracle." *Ladies' Home Journal,* August 1990, p. 99.

Fest, Marc. "Interview with Gloria Estefan." *Hörzu,* September 8, 1998, p. 118.

Genz, Michelle. "Golden Girl." *Miami Herald,* May 31, 1998, Tropic Section, p. 10.

Gerosa, Melina. "Gloria's Greatest Hits." *Ladies' Home Journal,* August 1996, p. 40.

Gonzalez, Fernando. "Air Gloria! Singer to Miami: 'It's Our Party.'" *Miami Herald,* September 21, 1996, p. 1A.

Johnson, Richard. "Sweet Revenge." *New York Post,* January 30, 1999, p. 8.

Lane, Lynda. "Estefan, Others to Perform at Prez's Inaugural Gala." *Music Wire,* January 1997, <http://www.musicblvd.com/cgibin/tw/14940250914858158_105_821195^s&> (August 1, 1999).

Levin, Jordan. "A Cuban Fantasía Mambos into Main Street." *New York Times,* November 16, 1997, Section IX, p. 3.

"Make a Difference Next Saturday." *USA Weekend,* October 16, 1998, pp. 4–5.

Martin, Lydia. "Evolution of Pop Diva Transcends Power, Fame." *Miami Herald,* September 15, 1996, p. 1L.

McLane, Daisann. "The Power and the Gloria." *Rolling Stone,* June 14, 1990, p. 74.

Morse, Steve. "Gloria Estefan Brings Her Audiences Together." *Boston Globe,* May 31, 1996, p. 61.

Pitts, Leonard Jr. "Hurricane Relief." *Miami Herald,* September 25, 1992, p. 22G.

TELEVISION SHOWS

CBS This Morning. CBS, November 4, 1998. Interview of Gloria by Mark McEwen.

"Gloria Estefan: Intimate Portrait." Lifetime Television Network, broadcast January 6, 1997.

"Live by Request." A&E Television Network, broadcast November 3, 1998.

GOVERNMENT RECORDS

Florida House of Representatives Full Committee on Natural Resources, hearing, February 7, 1996.

ELECTRONIC MEDIA

Various Internet Web sites, including:
Celebsite: Gloria Estefan
    <http://www.celsite.com/people/gloriaestefan>
Gloria Estefan Online <http://www.estefan.net>
LatinoLink <http://www.latinolink.com>
The Official Gloria Estefan Web Site <http://www.gloriafan.com>
U.S. News for German Media
    <http://www.fest.net/marc/estefan>
Women's History Encyclopedia <http://www.teleport.com>

DISCOGRAPHY

ALBUMS AND CDS

Renacer (1977, independent. Re-released with new sleeve as *Live Again.)*

Miami Sound Machine (1978, independent. Released in both Spanish and English editions.)

Imported (1979, independent)

MSM (1980, Discos CBS International)

Otra Vez (1981, CBS)

Río (1982, CBS)

Lo Mejor de Miami Sound Machine (1983, CBS)

A Toda Máquina (1984, CBS)

Eyes of Innocence (1984, Epic Records)

Primitive Love (1985, Epic)

Let it Loose (1987, Epic. Also released as *Anything for You.)*

Cuts Both Ways (1989, Epic)

Exitos de Gloria Estefan (1990, Epic)

Into the Light (1991, Epic)

Greatest Hits (1992, Epic)

Mi Tierra (1993, Epic)

Christmas Through Your Eyes (1993, Epic)

Hold Me, Thrill Me, Kiss Me (1994, Epic)

Abriendo Puertas (1995, Epic)

Destiny (1996, Epic)

gloria! (1998, Epic)

(Numbers in parenthesis include the year the single was released and its peak chart position according to *Billboard* magazine.)

MIAMI SOUND MACHINE

Conga (1986, 10)

Bad Boy (1986, 8)

Words Get in the Way (1986, 5)

Falling in Love (Uh-Oh) (1987, 25)

GLORIA ESTEFAN AND THE MIAMI SOUND MACHINE

Rhythm Is Gonna Get You (1987, 5)

Betcha Say That (1987, 36)

Can't Stay Away from You (1988, 6)

Anything for You (1988, 1)

1-2-3 (1988, 2)

GLORIA ESTEFAN

Don't Wanna Lose You (1989, 1)

Get on Your Feet (1989, 11)

Here We Are (1990, 6)

Cuts Both Ways (1990, —)

Oye Mi Canto (Hear My Voice) (1990, —)

Coming out of the Dark (1991, 1)

Live for Loving You (1991, 22)

Can't Forget You (1991, —)

Seal Our Fate (1991, —)

Always Tomorrow (1992, —)

I See Your Smile (1993, —)

Turn the Beat Around (1994, 13)

Everlasting Love (1995, 27)

Reach (1996, 15)

You'll Be Mine (Party Time) (1996, —)

I'm Not Giving You Up (1997, 23)

Heaven's What I Feel (1998, 9)

VIDEOGRAPHY

Video Exitos (1986)

Homecoming Concert (1989)

Evolution (1990)

Coming out of the Dark (1990)

Into the Light World Tour (1991)

Everlasting Gloria (1995)

Evolution Tour '96: Live in Miami (1996)

Don't Stop (1998)

INDEX

OTHER TITLES FROM LERNER AND A&E®:

Arthur Ashe
Bill Gates
Bruce Lee
Chief Crazy Horse
Christopher Reeve
George Lucas
Jacques Cousteau
Jesse Owens
Jesse Ventura
John Glenn
Legends of Dracula
Louisa May Alcott

Madeleine Albright
Maya Angelou
Mother Teresa
Nelson Mandela
Princess Diana
Queen Cleopatra
Rosie O'Donnell
Saint Joan of Arc
Wilma Rudolph
Women in Space
Women of the Wild West

ABOUT THE AUTHOR

Michael Benson, originally from Rochester, New York, received his bachelor's degree in Communication Arts from Hofstra University. He is the author of fourteen books, covering topics from science fiction films to monster trucks. He currently works as a magazine editor and lives in Brooklyn, New York, with his wife and children.

PHOTO ACKNOWLEDGMENTS

© George Bodnar/Retna Ltd., pp. 2, 72; AP/Wide World Photos, pp. 6, 28, 34, 38, 44, 46, 48, 55, 62, 64, 74, 77, 79, 85; American Stock/Archive Photos, p. 9; Corbis, p. 12; Seth Poppel Yearbook Archives, pp. 13, 16; © Gary Gershoff/Retna Ltd., p. 19; © Troy/Retna Ltd., p. 22; © John Barret/Globe Photos, Inc., pp. 24, 37; © Govert de Roos/Sunshine/Retna Ltd., p. 32; © Scott Weiner/Retna Ltd., p. 40; Richard Corkery/New York Daily News, p. 51; © Michael Ferguson/Globe Photos, p. 56; © Barry Talesnick/Retna Ltd., p. 68; Freddy Baez/Archive Photos, p. 69; Reuters/Gary Hershorn/Archive Photos, p. 70; © Stills Press Agency/Retna Ltd., p. 80; © Walter McBride/Retna Ltd., p. 88; Reuters/Jeff Christensen/Archive Photos, p. 93; © Dave Benett/Globe Photos, Inc., p. 96; Reuters/Andy Clark/Archive Photos, p. 98.

Cover photos (hard cover and paperback)
© Steve Granitz/Retna Ltd., front; © George Bodnar/Retna Ltd., back.